MW00423419

Thank you for purchasing this PMDD journal! Firstly, let me introduce myself, and later I'll explain a little about the book and how to use it.

I am Joanne and I have suffered with PMDD for a while now. I struggled for years with symptoms that affected me both physically and mentally, but it was only when I started tracking my symptoms that I made the connection with my cycle and was able to put a name to the illness and seek help. Along my journey I have tried a great many products & techniques to alleviate symptoms – some helpful, some not so much, but one of the *most pivotal* things to do is to **track**! Of course there are so many tracking apps to choose from that have some amazing features. They can tell you what day of your cycle you're on, record the data you input and even notice the patterns for you. I would definitely recommend using any of these apps alongside this journal.

The reason I have created a paper journal is because apps are on phones, and phones are distracting. I hate this age we live in where everyone is addicted to technology and I make as much effort as I can to move away from my phone and avoid getting sucked in! I also personally find that actually writing with a pen instead of typing on a keyboard is more therapeutic and meaningful. The words seem to leave me as they appear on the page, and this can be really useful for the worst days. It's like emptying my brain...

I hope I have included the important questions that will help you to track your symptoms, and that this book will prove useful for Doctors' appointments, or a way of unloading onto paper. It's pretty self-explanatory, and you can use the areas however works best for you, but I've included a little "How-To" below to help get you started.

If I help just one person with this book, I'll be satisfied.

Best of luck!

How To - Fill the book out at the end of each day so that you can look back on the day.

Day of cycle: The first day of your period is day one. The day before your next period is the last day of your cycle, and you will ovulate somewhere in the middle. If it helps, start keeping the journal on day one.

General Mood: Tick or circle the face that depicts your mood, or draw your own in "Other".

Appointments: Keep a note of any Doctor's or Gynaecologist appointments in here or use it as a reminder for when tablets are going to run out to call your Doctor & order new ones.

Medication / Supplements Taken Today: Logging what you've taken is a good reminder for you if you've forgotten to take a tablet, and helps to track if there is any correlation between new medication and the effect on your symptoms.

Food diary: Tracking your food may help weed out those trigger foods. Even if you only write down foods you believe to be triggering symptoms, you may notice a pattern. I would recommend logging all meals to begin with.

Rate your symptoms: Give your symptoms a rating; either from 1-5 or 1-10 – whichever works best for you. There's space to add your own symptoms, too.

List some activities: This is important so that you can see if there is anything triggering moods or, on the flip side, anything that makes you feel better.

List 5 things you're grateful for today: Getting your brain into a state of gratitude is actually a big game changer. As a sufferer, I know it's hard to get into that state but do try! At least if you're writing it, you may even begin to feel it...

Summarise your day: Use this space to vent, to rant or to just get your thoughts out there on paper. This is a free writing space and yours for whatever you feel you want to write. Draw a picture, scribble, and write your thoughts or whatever you like!

Day of cycle: 28? Date: 01./.08/.2023

General Mood:

Other

OK / Happy   Unsure / Not Great   Angry / Raging   Emotional

Appointments / things to do today:	•
• Gym	•
• BRING SHOES TO STORE	•
•	•
	•

Medication / supplements taken today:

℞ Zoloft

| Breakfast NOTHING | Lunch HAMBURGER |
| Dinner FROZEN PIZZA | Snacks TEA LATTE |

Rate your worst symptoms today:

Anger ☐ Anxiety ☑ De-Motivation ☐ Depression ☐ Insomnia ☐
Irritability ☑ Misophonia ☐ Paranoia ☐ Teary ☑ Other:
.... ☐ .... ☐ .... ☐ .... ☐ .... ☐

PARKER: mood → Emotional + Happy
Symptoms → Anxious,

CHecked google a few times within a week

List some activities you did today:

- Went to the gym
- Visited a friend for a bit
- Played a game with parker
- Went to the store
- Watched Netflix show

List at least 5 things you're grateful for today:

- The nice weather
- affordable resource to excersize
- Supporting family
-
-

Summarise your day and how you're feeling:

My day was off and on. I was either in a really good mood or feeling pretty emotional. Still overthinking health / doctors results. Last day of my vacation, feeling a little anxious and not really feeling refreshed from the break.

Day of cycle: 29   Date: 01/03/2023

General Mood:

Other

OK / Happy   Unsure /   Angry /   Emotional   worried
               Not Great   Raging

Appointments / things to do today:	
• Groceries • Work •	• • • • •

Medication / supplements taken today:

Zoloft   max WALKING: 118
                    bpm: 146
                    resting: 59

Breakfast banana bread breakfast wrap	Lunch Tex - mex rice bowl
Dinner wrap + half ham burger	Snacks Coffee

Rate your worst symptoms today:

Anger ☐ Anxiety ☑ De-Motivation ☐ Depression ☐ Insomnia ☑
Irritability ☐ Misophonia ☐ Paranoia ☑ Teary ☐ Other:
.... ☐ .... ☐ .... ☐ .... ☐ .... ☐

List some activities you did today:

- I made supper from scratch
- worked
- Visited parkers parents
- Groceries

List at least 5 things you're grateful for today:

- That I ate healthy
- Kind coworkers
- Clean pss
-
-

Summarise your day and how you're feeling:

I felt overall pretty good aside from my 15 min + 30 min break. I got a urine sample / STD test and Im having really bad paranoia and anxiety about the results even though I've had the same partner. I called 811, Pharmacy, Doctor, and did a lot of research due to this anxiety.

Parker: neutral.

Day of cycle: Date: ..../......./.........

General Mood: Other

OK / Happy   Unsure /   Angry /   Emotional
                    Not Great   Raging

Appointments / things to do today:	
• • •	• • • • •
Medication / supplements taken today:	
Breakfast	Lunch

Rate your worst symptoms today:

Anger ☐ Anxiety ☐ De-Motivation ☐ Depression ☐ Insomnia ☐

Irritability ☐ Misophonia ☐ Paranoia ☐ Teary ☐ Other:

...............☐ ....☐ ....☐ ....☐ ....☐

List some activities you did today:

List at least 5 things you're grateful for today:

-
-
-
-
-

Summarise your day and how you're feeling:

Day of cycle: Date: ..../......./.........

General Mood:
                                                            Other

OK / Happy   Unsure /   Angry /   Emotional
                  Not Great   Raging

Appointments / things to do today:	•
•	•
•	•
•	•
	•

Medication / supplements taken today:

| Breakfast | Lunch |

Rate your worst symptoms today:

Anger ☐ Anxiety ☐ De-Motivation ☐ Depression ☐ Insomnia ☐
Irritability ☐ Misophonia ☐ Paranoia ☐ Teary ☐ Other:

................☐ ....☐ ....☐ ....☐ ....☐

List some activities you did today:

List at least 5 things you're grateful for today:

-
-
-
-
-

Summarise your day and how you're feeling:

Day of cycle: Date: ..../......./.........

General Mood:
                                                              Other

OK / Happy   Unsure /   Angry /   Emotional
                Not Great   Raging

Appointments / things to do today:	
 • • •	• • • • •
Medication / supplements taken today:	
Breakfast	Lunch

Rate your worst symptoms today:

Anger ☐ Anxiety ☐ De-Motivation ☐ Depression ☐ Insomnia ☐
Irritability ☐ Misophonia ☐ Paranoia ☐ Teary ☐ Other:

............☐ ....☐ ....☐ ....☐ ....☐

List some activities you did today:

List at least 5 things you're grateful for today:

-
-
-
-
-

Summarise your day and how you're feeling:

Day of cycle: Date: ……./……./………

General Mood: Other

OK / Happy	Unsure / Not Great	Angry / Raging	Emotional	

Appointments / things to do today:	
• • •	• • • • •
Medication / supplements taken today:	
Breakfast	Lunch

Rate your worst symptoms today:

Anger ☐ Anxiety ☐ De-Motivation ☐ Depression ☐ Insomnia ☐
Irritability ☐ Misophonia ☐ Paranoia ☐ Teary ☐ Other:

…………… ☐ ……………… ☐ …………… ☐ …………… ☐ ……………… ☐

List some activities you did today:

List at least 5 things you're grateful for today:

-
-
-
-
-

Summarise your day and how you're feeling:

Day of cycle: Date: ..../......./.........

General Mood: Other

OK / Happy   Unsure /   Angry /   Emotional
                  Not Great   Raging

Appointments / things to do today:	
• • •	• • • • •
Medication / supplements taken today:	
Breakfast	Lunch

Rate your worst symptoms today:

Anger ☐ Anxiety ☐ De-Motivation ☐ Depression ☐ Insomnia ☐
Irritability ☐ Misophonia ☐ Paranoia ☐ Teary ☐ Other:

..............☐ ....☐ ....☐ ....☐ ....☐

List some activities you did today:

List at least 5 things you're grateful for today:

-
-
-
-
-

Summarise your day and how you're feeling:

Day of cycle: _____   Date: ..../......./........

General Mood:

                                                              Other

OK / Happy   Unsure /   Angry /   Emotional
                  Not Great   Raging

Appointments / things to do today:	
• • •	• • • • •

Medication / supplements taken today:

Breakfast	Lunch

Rate your worst symptoms today:

Anger ☐ Anxiety ☐ De-Motivation ☐ Depression ☐ Insomnia ☐
Irritability ☐ Misophonia ☐ Paranoia ☐ Teary ☐ Other:

.... ☐ .... ☐ .... ☐ .... ☐ .... ☐

List some activities you did today:

List at least 5 things you're grateful for today:

-
-
-
-
-

Summarise your day and how you're feeling:

Day of cycle: Date: ..../......./.........

General Mood: Other

OK / Happy   Unsure /   Angry /   Emotional
                Not Great   Raging

Appointments / things to do today:	
• • •	• • • • •

Medication / supplements taken today:

Breakfast	Lunch

Rate your worst symptoms today:

Anger ☐ Anxiety ☐ De-Motivation ☐ Depression ☐ Insomnia ☐
Irritability ☐ Misophonia ☐ Paranoia ☐ Teary ☐ Other:

................☐ ....☐ ....☐ ....☐ ....☐

List some activities you did today:

List at least 5 things you're grateful for today:

-
-
-
-
-

Summarise your day and how you're feeling:

Day of cycle: Date: ..../......./.........

General Mood: Other

OK / Happy   Unsure /   Angry /   Emotional
                  Not Great   Raging

Appointments / things to do today:	
• • •	• • • • •

Medication / supplements taken today:

Breakfast	Lunch

Rate your worst symptoms today:

Anger ☐ Anxiety ☐ De-Motivation ☐ Depression ☐ Insomnia ☐
Irritability ☐ Misophonia ☐ Paranoia ☐ Teary ☐ Other:

.................☐ ....☐ ....☐ ....☐ ....☐

List some activities you did today:

List at least 5 things you're grateful for today:

-
-
-
-
-

Summarise your day and how you're feeling:

Day of cycle: Date: ..../......./........

General Mood:

Other

OK / Happy   Unsure /   Angry /   Emotional
                  Not Great   Raging

Appointments / things to do today:	
• • •	• • • • •

Medication / supplements taken today:

Breakfast	Lunch

Rate your worst symptoms today:

Anger ☐ Anxiety ☐ De-Motivation ☐ Depression ☐ Insomnia ☐
Irritability ☐ Misophonia ☐ Paranoia ☐ Teary ☐ Other:

.............☐ ....☐ ....☐ ....☐ ....☐

List some activities you did today:

List at least 5 things you're grateful for today:

-
-
-
-
-

Summarise your day and how you're feeling:

Day of cycle: Date: ..../......./........

General Mood: Other

OK / Happy	Unsure / Not Great	Angry / Raging	Emotional	

Appointments / things to do today:	•
• • •	• • • •

Medication / supplements taken today:

Breakfast	Lunch

Rate your worst symptoms today:

Anger ☐ Anxiety ☐ De-Motivation ☐ Depression ☐ Insomnia ☐

Irritability ☐ Misophonia ☐ Paranoia ☐ Teary ☐ Other:

............☐ ....☐ ....☐ ....☐ ....☐

List some activities you did today:

List at least 5 things you're grateful for today:

-
-
-
-
-

Summarise your day and how you're feeling:

Day of cycle: Date: ..../......./........

General Mood:
                                                   Other

OK / Happy   Unsure /   Angry /   Emotional
                  Not Great   Raging

Appointments / things to do today:	• • • • •
• • •	

Medication / supplements taken today:

Breakfast	Lunch

Rate your worst symptoms today:

Anger ☐ Anxiety ☐ De-Motivation ☐ Depression ☐ Insomnia ☐
Irritability ☐ Misophonia ☐ Paranoia ☐ Teary ☐ Other:

..............☐ ....☐ ....☐ ....☐ ....☐

List some activities you did today:

List at least 5 things you're grateful for today:

-
-
-
-
-

Summarise your day and how you're feeling:

Day of cycle: Date: ..../......./........

General Mood:

Other

OK / Happy   Unsure /   Angry /   Emotional
                  Not Great   Raging

Appointments / things to do today:	
• • •	• • • • •
Medication / supplements taken today:	
Breakfast	Lunch

Rate your worst symptoms today:

Anger ☐ Anxiety ☐ De-Motivation ☐ Depression ☐ Insomnia ☐
Irritability ☐ Misophonia ☐ Paranoia ☐ Teary ☐ Other:

................☐ ....☐ ....☐ ....☐ ....☐

List some activities you did today:

List at least 5 things you're grateful for today:

-
-
-
-
-

Summarise your day and how you're feeling:

Day of cycle: Date: ..../......./........

General Mood: Other

OK / Happy   Unsure /   Angry /   Emotional
                    Not Great   Raging

Appointments / things to do today:	
• • •	• • • • •
Medication / supplements taken today:	
Breakfast	Lunch

Rate your worst symptoms today:

Anger ☐ Anxiety ☐ De-Motivation ☐ Depression ☐ Insomnia ☐

Irritability ☐ Misophonia ☐ Paranoia ☐ Teary ☐ Other:

................☐ ....☐ ....☐ ....☐ ....☐

List some activities you did today:

List at least 5 things you're grateful for today:

-
-
-
-
-

Summarise your day and how you're feeling:

Day of cycle: Date: ..../......./........

General Mood:

                                                           Other

OK / Happy	Unsure / Not Great	Angry / Raging	Emotional	

Appointments / things to do today:	•
• • •	• • • •

Medication / supplements taken today:	

Breakfast	Lunch

Rate your worst symptoms today:

Anger ☐ Anxiety ☐ De-Motivation ☐ Depression ☐ Insomnia ☐
Irritability ☐ Misophonia ☐ Paranoia ☐ Teary ☐ Other:

............☐ ....☐ ....☐ ....☐ ....☐

List some activities you did today:

List at least 5 things you're grateful for today:

-
-
-
-
-

Summarise your day and how you're feeling:

Day of cycle: _____   Date: ..../......./........

General Mood: Other

OK / Happy   Unsure /   Angry /   Emotional   [   ]
                    Not Great   Raging

Appointments / things to do today:	
• • •	• • • • •
Medication / supplements taken today:	
Breakfast	Lunch

Rate your worst symptoms today:

Anger ☐ Anxiety ☐ De-Motivation ☐ Depression ☐ Insomnia ☐
Irritability ☐ Misophonia ☐ Paranoia ☐ Teary ☐ Other:

.... ☐ .... ☐ .... ☐ .... ☐ .... ☐

List some activities you did today:

List at least 5 things you're grateful for today:

-
-
-
-
-

Summarise your day and how you're feeling:

Day of cycle: _____   Date: ..../......./.........

General Mood:

Other

OK / Happy   Unsure /   Angry /   Emotional
                Not Great   Raging

Appointments / things to do today:	•
• • •	• • •

Medication / supplements taken today:

Breakfast	Lunch

Rate your worst symptoms today:

Anger ☐ Anxiety ☐ De-Motivation ☐ Depression ☐ Insomnia ☐

Irritability ☐ Misophonia ☐ Paranoia ☐ Teary ☐ Other:

.............☐ ....☐ ....☐ ....☐ ....☐

List some activities you did today:

List at least 5 things you're grateful for today:

-
-
-
-
-

Summarise your day and how you're feeling:

Day of cycle: Date: ..../......./.........

General Mood: Other

OK / Happy   Unsure /   Angry /   Emotional
                    Not Great   Raging

Appointments / things to do today:	•
• • •	• • • •

Medication / supplements taken today:

Breakfast	Lunch

Rate your worst symptoms today:

Anger ☐ Anxiety ☐ De-Motivation ☐ Depression ☐ Insomnia ☐
Irritability ☐ Misophonia ☐ Paranoia ☐ Teary ☐ Other:

.... ☐ .... ☐ .... ☐ .... ☐ .... ☐

List some activities you did today:

List at least 5 things you're grateful for today:

-
-
-
-
-

Summarise your day and how you're feeling:

Day of cycle: Date: ..../......./........

General Mood:

                                                              Other

OK / Happy   Unsure /   Angry /   Emotional
               Not Great   Raging

Appointments / things to do today:	
• • •	• • • • •
Medication / supplements taken today:	
Breakfast	Lunch

Rate your worst symptoms today:

Anger ☐ Anxiety ☐ De-Motivation ☐ Depression ☐ Insomnia ☐
Irritability ☐ Misophonia ☐ Paranoia ☐ Teary ☐ Other:

...............☐ ....☐ ....☐ ....☐ ....☐

List some activities you did today:

List at least 5 things you're grateful for today:

-
-
-
-
-

Summarise your day and how you're feeling:

Day of cycle: Date: ..../......./.........

General Mood: Other

OK / Happy   Unsure /   Angry /   Emotional
                  Not Great   Raging

Appointments / things to do today:	
• • •	• • • • •

Medication / supplements taken today:

Breakfast	Lunch

Rate your worst symptoms today:

Anger ☐ Anxiety ☐ De-Motivation ☐ Depression ☐ Insomnia ☐
Irritability ☐ Misophonia ☐ Paranoia ☐ Teary ☐ Other:

................☐ ....☐ ....☐ ....☐ ....☐

List some activities you did today:

List at least 5 things you're grateful for today:

-
-
-
-
-

Summarise your day and how you're feeling:

Day of cycle: Date: ..../......./.........

General Mood: Other

OK / Happy   Unsure /   Angry /   Emotional
                  Not Great   Raging

Appointments / things to do today:	
• • •	• • • • •

Medication / supplements taken today:

Breakfast	Lunch

Rate your worst symptoms today:

Anger ☐ Anxiety ☐ De-Motivation ☐ Depression ☐ Insomnia ☐
Irritability ☐ Misophonia ☐ Paranoia ☐ Teary ☐ Other:

................☐ ....☐ ....☐ ....☐ ....☐

List some activities you did today:

List at least 5 things you're grateful for today:

-
-
-
-
-

Summarise your day and how you're feeling:

Day of cycle: _____   Date: ..../......./........

General Mood:

                                                                    Other

OK / Happy   Unsure /   Angry /   Emotional
                Not Great   Raging

Appointments / things to do today: · · ·	· · · · ·
Medication / supplements taken today:	
Breakfast	Lunch

Rate your worst symptoms today:

Anger ☐ Anxiety ☐ De-Motivation ☐ Depression ☐ Insomnia ☐
Irritability ☐ Misophonia ☐ Paranoia ☐ Teary ☐ Other:

...............☐ ....☐ ....☐ ....☐ ....☐

List some activities you did today:

List at least 5 things you're grateful for today:

-
-
-
-
-

Summarise your day and how you're feeling:

Day of cycle: Date: ..../......./.........

General Mood: Other

OK / Happy	Unsure / Not Great	Angry / Raging	Emotional	

Appointments / things to do today:	
• • •	• • • • •

Medication / supplements taken today:

Breakfast	Lunch

Rate your worst symptoms today:

Anger ☐ Anxiety ☐ De-Motivation ☐ Depression ☐ Insomnia ☐
Irritability ☐ Misophonia ☐ Paranoia ☐ Teary ☐ Other:

.............☐ ....☐ ....☐ ....☐ ....☐

List some activities you did today:

List at least 5 things you're grateful for today:

-
-
-
-
-

Summarise your day and how you're feeling:

Day of cycle: Date: ..../......./.........

General Mood:
                                                     Other

OK / Happy   Unsure /   Angry /   Emotional
                  Not Great   Raging

Appointments / things to do today: • • •	• • • • •
Medication / supplements taken today:	
Breakfast	Lunch

Rate your worst symptoms today:

Anger ☐ Anxiety ☐ De-Motivation ☐ Depression ☐ Insomnia ☐
Irritability ☐ Misophonia ☐ Paranoia ☐ Teary ☐ Other:

...............☐ ....☐ ....☐ ....☐ ....☐

List some activities you did today:

List at least 5 things you're grateful for today:

-
-
-
-
-

Summarise your day and how you're feeling:

Day of cycle: _____   Date: ..../......./........

General Mood:

Other

OK / Happy   Unsure /   Angry /   Emotional
                Not Great   Raging

Appointments / things to do today:	
• • •	• • • • •

Medication / supplements taken today:

Breakfast	Lunch

Rate your worst symptoms today:

Anger ☐ Anxiety ☐ De-Motivation ☐ Depression ☐ Insomnia ☐
Irritability ☐ Misophonia ☐ Paranoia ☐ Teary ☐ Other:

............☐ ....☐ ....☐ ....☐ ....☐

List some activities you did today:

List at least 5 things you're grateful for today:

-
-
-
-
-

Summarise your day and how you're feeling:

Day of cycle: Date: ..../......./.........

General Mood: Other

OK / Happy   Unsure /   Angry /   Emotional
                  Not Great   Raging

Appointments / things to do today:	•
• • •	• • • •

Medication / supplements taken today:

Breakfast	Lunch

Rate your worst symptoms today:

Anger ☐ Anxiety ☐ De-Motivation ☐ Depression ☐ Insomnia ☐
Irritability ☐ Misophonia ☐ Paranoia ☐ Teary ☐ Other:

...............☐ ....☐ ....☐ ....☐ ....☐

List some activities you did today:

List at least 5 things you're grateful for today:

-
-
-
-
-

Summarise your day and how you're feeling:

Day of cycle: Date: ..../......./.........

General Mood:
                                                              Other

OK / Happy   Unsure /   Angry /   Emotional
                  Not Great   Raging

Appointments / things to do today:	• • • • •
• • •	
Medication / supplements taken today:	
Breakfast	Lunch

Rate your worst symptoms today:

Anger ☐ Anxiety ☐ De-Motivation ☐ Depression ☐ Insomnia ☐
Irritability ☐ Misophonia ☐ Paranoia ☐ Teary ☐ Other:

................☐ ....☐ ....☐ ....☐ ....☐

List some activities you did today:

List at least 5 things you're grateful for today:

-
-
-
-
-

Summarise your day and how you're feeling:

Day of cycle: Date: ..../......./........

General Mood: Other

OK / Happy   Unsure /   Angry /   Emotional
                    Not Great   Raging

Appointments / things to do today:	•
•	•
•	•
•	•
	•
Medication / supplements taken today:	
Breakfast	Lunch

Rate your worst symptoms today:

Anger ☐ Anxiety ☐ De-Motivation ☐ Depression ☐ Insomnia ☐
Irritability ☐ Misophonia ☐ Paranoia ☐ Teary ☐ Other:

................☐ ....☐ ....☐ ....☐ ....☐

List some activities you did today:

List at least 5 things you're grateful for today:

-
-
-
-
-

Summarise your day and how you're feeling:

Day of cycle: Date: ..../......./.........

General Mood: Other

OK / Happy   Unsure /   Angry /   Emotional
                Not Great   Raging

Appointments / things to do today:	
• • •	• • • • •

Medication / supplements taken today:

Breakfast	Lunch

Rate your worst symptoms today:

Anger ☐ Anxiety ☐ De-Motivation ☐ Depression ☐ Insomnia ☐
Irritability ☐ Misophonia ☐ Paranoia ☐ Teary ☐ Other:

................☐ ....☐ ....☐ ....☐ ....☐

List some activities you did today:

List at least 5 things you're grateful for today:

-
-
-
-
-

Summarise your day and how you're feeling:

Day of cycle: Date: ..../......./.........

General Mood: Other

OK / Happy   Unsure /   Angry /   Emotional
                  Not Great   Raging

Appointments / things to do today:	•
•	•
•	•
•	•
	•

Medication / supplements taken today:

Breakfast	Lunch

Rate your worst symptoms today:

Anger ☐ Anxiety ☐ De-Motivation ☐ Depression ☐ Insomnia ☐
Irritability ☐ Misophonia ☐ Paranoia ☐ Teary ☐ Other:

.... ☐ .... ☐ .... ☐ .... ☐ .... ☐

List some activities you did today:

List at least 5 things you're grateful for today:

-
-
-
-
-

Summarise your day and how you're feeling:

Day of cycle: Date: ..../......./........

General Mood:

Other

OK / Happy   Unsure /   Angry /   Emotional
                    Not Great   Raging

Appointments / things to do today:	
• • •	• • • • •

Medication / supplements taken today:

Breakfast	Lunch

Rate your worst symptoms today:

Anger ☐ Anxiety ☐ De-Motivation ☐ Depression ☐ Insomnia ☐
Irritability ☐ Misophonia ☐ Paranoia ☐ Teary ☐ Other:

............☐ ....☐ ....☐ ....☐ ....☐

List some activities you did today:

List at least 5 things you're grateful for today:

-
-
-
-
-

Summarise your day and how you're feeling:

Day of cycle: Date: ..../......./.........

General Mood: Other

OK / Happy   Unsure /   Angry /   Emotional
                  Not Great   Raging

Appointments / things to do today:	•
	•
	•
•	•
•	•
•	

Medication / supplements taken today:

| Breakfast | Lunch |

Rate your worst symptoms today:

Anger ☐ Anxiety ☐ De-Motivation ☐ Depression ☐ Insomnia ☐
Irritability ☐ Misophonia ☐ Paranoia ☐ Teary ☐ Other:

................☐ ....☐ ....☐ ....☐ ....☐

List some activities you did today:

List at least 5 things you're grateful for today:

-
-
-
-
-

Summarise your day and how you're feeling:

Day of cycle: Date: ..../......./.........

General Mood: Other

OK / Happy   Unsure /   Angry /   Emotional
                  Not Great   Raging

Appointments / things to do today:	•
• • •	• • • •

Medication / supplements taken today:

Breakfast	Lunch

Rate your worst symptoms today:

Anger ☐ Anxiety ☐ De-Motivation ☐ Depression ☐ Insomnia ☐
Irritability ☐ Misophonia ☐ Paranoia ☐ Teary ☐ Other:

...............☐ ....☐ ....☐ ....☐ ....☐

List some activities you did today:

List at least 5 things you're grateful for today:

-
-
-
-
-

Summarise your day and how you're feeling:

Day of cycle: Date: ..../......./.........

General Mood:

                                               Other

OK / Happy   Unsure / Not Great   Angry / Raging   Emotional

Appointments / things to do today:	
• • •	• • • • •
Medication / supplements taken today:	
Breakfast	Lunch

Rate your worst symptoms today:

Anger ☐ Anxiety ☐ De-Motivation ☐ Depression ☐ Insomnia ☐
Irritability ☐ Misophonia ☐ Paranoia ☐ Teary ☐ Other:

................☐ ....☐ ....☐ ....☐ ....☐

List some activities you did today:

List at least 5 things you're grateful for today:

-
-
-
-
-

Summarise your day and how you're feeling:

Day of cycle: Date: ..../......./.........

General Mood: Other

OK / Happy	Unsure / Not Great	Angry / Raging	Emotional	

Appointments / things to do today: • • •	• • • • •

Medication / supplements taken today:

Breakfast	Lunch

Rate your worst symptoms today:

Anger ☐ Anxiety ☐ De-Motivation ☐ Depression ☐ Insomnia ☐

Irritability ☐ Misophonia ☐ Paranoia ☐ Teary ☐ Other:

............☐ ....☐ ....☐ ....☐ ....☐

List some activities you did today:

List at least 5 things you're grateful for today:

-
-
-
-
-

Summarise your day and how you're feeling:

Day of cycle: Date: ..../......./.........

General Mood:

                                                       Other

OK / Happy	Unsure / Not Great	Angry / Raging	Emotional	

Appointments / things to do today: • • •	• • • • •

Medication / supplements taken today:

Breakfast	Lunch

Rate your worst symptoms today:

Anger ☐ Anxiety ☐ De-Motivation ☐ Depression ☐ Insomnia ☐
Irritability ☐ Misophonia ☐ Paranoia ☐ Teary ☐ Other:

................☐ ....☐ ....☐ ....☐ ....☐

List some activities you did today:

List at least 5 things you're grateful for today:

-
-
-
-
-

Summarise your day and how you're feeling:

Day of cycle: Date: ..../......./.........

General Mood:

                                                        Other

OK / Happy   Unsure /   Angry /   Emotional
                  Not Great   Raging

Appointments / things to do today:	•
•	•
•	•
•	•
	•

Medication / supplements taken today:

Breakfast	Lunch

Rate your worst symptoms today:

Anger ☐ Anxiety ☐ De-Motivation ☐ Depression ☐ Insomnia ☐
Irritability ☐ Misophonia ☐ Paranoia ☐ Teary ☐ Other:

...............☐ ....☐ ....☐ ....☐ ....☐

List some activities you did today:

List at least 5 things you're grateful for today:

-
-
-
-
-

Summarise your day and how you're feeling:

Day of cycle: Date: ..../......./.........

General Mood: Other

OK / Happy   Unsure /   Angry /   Emotional
                  Not Great   Raging

Appointments / things to do today:	•
•	•
•	•
•	•
	•
Medication / supplements taken today:	
Breakfast	Lunch

Rate your worst symptoms today:

Anger ☐ Anxiety ☐ De-Motivation ☐ Depression ☐ Insomnia ☐

Irritability ☐ Misophonia ☐ Paranoia ☐ Teary ☐ Other:

................☐ ....☐ ....☐ ....☐ ....☐

List some activities you did today:

List at least 5 things you're grateful for today:

-
-
-
-
-

Summarise your day and how you're feeling:

Day of cycle: Date: ..../......./.........

General Mood: Other

OK / Happy   Unsure /   Angry /   Emotional
                  Not Great   Raging

Appointments / things to do today:	• • • • •
• • •	

Medication / supplements taken today:

Breakfast	Lunch

Rate your worst symptoms today:

Anger ☐ Anxiety ☐ De-Motivation ☐ Depression ☐ Insomnia ☐

Irritability ☐ Misophonia ☐ Paranoia ☐ Teary ☐ Other:

...............☐ ....☐ ....☐ ....☐ ....☐

List some activities you did today:

List at least 5 things you're grateful for today:

-
-
-
-
-

Summarise your day and how you're feeling:

Day of cycle: Date: ..../......./.........

General Mood:

                                             Other

OK / Happy	Unsure / Not Great	Angry / Raging	Emotional	

Appointments / things to do today:	
• • •	• • • • •

Medication / supplements taken today:

Breakfast	Lunch

Rate your worst symptoms today:

Anger ☐ Anxiety ☐ De-Motivation ☐ Depression ☐ Insomnia ☐
Irritability ☐ Misophonia ☐ Paranoia ☐ Teary ☐ Other:

............☐ ....☐ ....☐ ....☐ ....☐

List some activities you did today:

List at least 5 things you're grateful for today:

-
-
-
-
-

Summarise your day and how you're feeling:

Day of cycle: Date: ..../......./.........

General Mood: Other

OK / Happy	Unsure / Not Great	Angry / Raging	Emotional	

Appointments / things to do today:	•
• • •	• • • •

Medication / supplements taken today:

Breakfast	Lunch

Rate your worst symptoms today:

Anger ☐ Anxiety ☐ De-Motivation ☐ Depression ☐ Insomnia ☐
Irritability ☐ Misophonia ☐ Paranoia ☐ Teary ☐ Other:

...............☐ ....☐ ....☐ ....☐ ....☐

List some activities you did today:

List at least 5 things you're grateful for today:

-
-
-
-
-

Summarise your day and how you're feeling:

Day of cycle: Date: ..../......./........

General Mood:

Other

OK / Happy   Unsure /   Angry /   Emotional
                  Not Great   Raging

Appointments / things to do today:	•
•	•
•	•
•	•

Medication / supplements taken today:

Breakfast	Lunch

Rate your worst symptoms today:

Anger ☐ Anxiety ☐ De-Motivation ☐ Depression ☐ Insomnia ☐
Irritability ☐ Misophonia ☐ Paranoia ☐ Teary ☐ Other:

...............☐ ....☐ ....☐ ....☐ ....☐

List some activities you did today:

List at least 5 things you're grateful for today:

-
-
-
-
-

Summarise your day and how you're feeling:

Day of cycle: Date: ..../......./........

General Mood:

                                                     Other

OK / Happy	Unsure / Not Great	Angry / Raging	Emotional	

Appointments / things to do today:	
• • •	• • • • •
Medication / supplements taken today:	
Breakfast	Lunch

Rate your worst symptoms today:

Anger ☐ Anxiety ☐ De-Motivation ☐ Depression ☐ Insomnia ☐
Irritability ☐ Misophonia ☐ Paranoia ☐ Teary ☐ Other:

.... ☐ .... ☐ .... ☐ .... ☐ .... ☐

List some activities you did today:

List at least 5 things you're grateful for today:

-
-
-
-
-

Summarise your day and how you're feeling:

Day of cycle: Date: ..../......./.........

General Mood: Other

OK / Happy   Unsure /   Angry /   Emotional
                    Not Great   Raging

Appointments / things to do today:	•
•	•
•	•
•	•

Medication / supplements taken today:

| Breakfast | Lunch |
| | |

Rate your worst symptoms today:

Anger ☐ Anxiety ☐ De-Motivation ☐ Depression ☐ Insomnia ☐
Irritability ☐ Misophonia ☐ Paranoia ☐ Teary ☐ Other:

................☐ ....☐ ....☐ ....☐ ....☐

List some activities you did today:

List at least 5 things you're grateful for today:

-
-
-
-
-

Summarise your day and how you're feeling:

Day of cycle: _____   Date: ..../......./.........

General Mood: Other

OK / Happy   Unsure /   Angry /   Emotional
                    Not Great   Raging

Appointments / things to do today:	
• • •	• • • • •
Medication / supplements taken today:	
Breakfast	**Lunch**

Rate your worst symptoms today:

Anger ☐ Anxiety ☐ De-Motivation ☐ Depression ☐ Insomnia ☐
Irritability ☐ Misophonia ☐ Paranoia ☐ Teary ☐ Other:

............☐ ....☐ ....☐ ....☐ ....☐

List some activities you did today:

List at least 5 things you're grateful for today:

-
-
-
-
-

Summarise your day and how you're feeling:

Day of cycle: Date: ..../......./.........

General Mood:

                                                        Other

OK / Happy   Unsure /   Angry /   Emotional
                  Not Great   Raging

Appointments / things to do today:	•
• • •	• • • •

Medication / supplements taken today:

Breakfast	Lunch

Rate your worst symptoms today:

Anger ☐ Anxiety ☐ De-Motivation ☐ Depression ☐ Insomnia ☐
Irritability ☐ Misophonia ☐ Paranoia ☐ Teary ☐ Other:

.............☐ ....☐ ....☐ ....☐ ....☐

List some activities you did today:

List at least 5 things you're grateful for today:

-
-
-
-
-

Summarise your day and how you're feeling:

Day of cycle: Date: ..../......./........

General Mood: Other

OK / Happy	Unsure / Not Great	Angry / Raging	Emotional	

Appointments / things to do today: • • •	• • • • •

Medication / supplements taken today:

Breakfast	Lunch

Rate your worst symptoms today:

Anger ☐ Anxiety ☐ De-Motivation ☐ Depression ☐ Insomnia ☐
Irritability ☐ Misophonia ☐ Paranoia ☐ Teary ☐ Other:

................☐ ....☐ ....☐ ....☐ ....☐

List some activities you did today:

List at least 5 things you're grateful for today:

-
-
-
-
-

Summarise your day and how you're feeling:

Day of cycle: Date: ..../......./........

General Mood:

                                                                Other

OK / Happy   Unsure /   Angry /   Emotional
                  Not Great   Raging

Appointments / things to do today:	•
•	•
•	•
•	•
	•

Medication / supplements taken today:

Breakfast	Lunch

Rate your worst symptoms today:

Anger ☐ Anxiety ☐ De-Motivation ☐ Depression ☐ Insomnia ☐
Irritability ☐ Misophonia ☐ Paranoia ☐ Teary ☐ Other:

.... ☐ .... ☐ .... ☐ .... ☐ .... ☐

List some activities you did today:

List at least 5 things you're grateful for today:

-
-
-
-
-

Summarise your day and how you're feeling:

Day of cycle: Date: ..../......./.........

General Mood:

                                         Other

OK / Happy   Unsure /   Angry /   Emotional
               Not Great   Raging

Appointments / things to do today:	
• • •	• • • • •
Medication / supplements taken today:	
Breakfast	Lunch

Rate your worst symptoms today:

Anger ☐ Anxiety ☐ De-Motivation ☐ Depression ☐ Insomnia ☐
Irritability ☐ Misophonia ☐ Paranoia ☐ Teary ☐ Other:

...............☐ ....☐ ....☐ ....☐ ....☐

List some activities you did today:

List at least 5 things you're grateful for today:

-
-
-
-
-

Summarise your day and how you're feeling:

Day of cycle: Date: ..../......./.........

General Mood:
                                                      Other

OK / Happy   Unsure /   Angry /   Emotional
                 Not Great   Raging

Appointments / things to do today:	
• • •	• • • • •

Medication / supplements taken today:

Breakfast	Lunch

Rate your worst symptoms today:

Anger ☐ Anxiety ☐ De-Motivation ☐ Depression ☐ Insomnia ☐
Irritability ☐ Misophonia ☐ Paranoia ☐ Teary ☐ Other:

...............☐ ....☐ ....☐ ....☐ ....☐

List some activities you did today:

List at least 5 things you're grateful for today:

-
-
-
-
-

Summarise your day and how you're feeling:

Day of cycle: Date: ..../......./.........

General Mood:

                                                 Other

OK / Happy   Unsure /   Angry /   Emotional
                Not Great   Raging

Appointments / things to do today: • • •	• • • • •
Medication / supplements taken today:	
Breakfast	Lunch

Rate your worst symptoms today:

Anger ☐ Anxiety ☐ De-Motivation ☐ Depression ☐ Insomnia ☐
Irritability ☐ Misophonia ☐ Paranoia ☐ Teary ☐ Other:

...............☐ ....☐ ....☐ ....☐ ....☐

List some activities you did today:

List at least 5 things you're grateful for today:

-
-
-
-
-

Summarise your day and how you're feeling:

Day of cycle: Date: ..../......./........

General Mood: Other

OK / Happy   Unsure /   Angry /   Emotional
                Not Great   Raging

Appointments / things to do today:	
• • •	• • • • •

Medication / supplements taken today:

Breakfast	Lunch

Rate your worst symptoms today:

Anger ☐ Anxiety ☐ De-Motivation ☐ Depression ☐ Insomnia ☐
Irritability ☐ Misophonia ☐ Paranoia ☐ Teary ☐ Other:

................☐ ....☐ ....☐ ....☐ ....☐

List some activities you did today:

List at least 5 things you're grateful for today:

-
-
-
-
-

Summarise your day and how you're feeling:

Day of cycle: Date: ..../......./........

General Mood: Other

OK / Happy   Unsure /   Angry /   Emotional
                  Not Great   Raging

Appointments / things to do today:	
• • •	• • • • •
Medication / supplements taken today:	
Breakfast	Lunch

Rate your worst symptoms today:

Anger ☐ Anxiety ☐ De-Motivation ☐ Depression ☐ Insomnia ☐

Irritability ☐ Misophonia ☐ Paranoia ☐ Teary ☐ Other:

.... ☐ .... ☐ .... ☐ .... ☐ .... ☐

List some activities you did today:

List at least 5 things you're grateful for today:

-
-
-
-
-

Summarise your day and how you're feeling:

Day of cycle: Date: ..../......./........

General Mood: Other

OK / Happy   Unsure /   Angry /   Emotional
                  Not Great   Raging

Appointments / things to do today:	
• • •	• • • • •

Medication / supplements taken today:

Breakfast	Lunch

Rate your worst symptoms today:

Anger ☐ Anxiety ☐ De-Motivation ☐ Depression ☐ Insomnia ☐
Irritability ☐ Misophonia ☐ Paranoia ☐ Teary ☐ Other:

............☐ ....☐ ....☐ ....☐ ....☐

List some activities you did today:

List at least 5 things you're grateful for today:

-
-
-
-
-

Summarise your day and how you're feeling:

Day of cycle: Date: ..../......./........

General Mood:

Other

OK / Happy   Unsure /   Angry /   Emotional
                    Not Great   Raging

Appointments / things to do today:	
• • •	• • • • •
Medication / supplements taken today:	
Breakfast	Lunch

Rate your worst symptoms today:

Anger ☐ Anxiety ☐ De-Motivation ☐ Depression ☐ Insomnia ☐
Irritability ☐ Misophonia ☐ Paranoia ☐ Teary ☐ Other:

.... ☐ .... ☐ .... ☐ .... ☐ .... ☐

List some activities you did today:

List at least 5 things you're grateful for today:

-
-
-
-
-

Summarise your day and how you're feeling:

Day of cycle: Date: ..../......./........

General Mood: Other

OK / Happy   Unsure /   Angry /   Emotional
              Not Great   Raging

Appointments / things to do today:	
• • •	• • • • •
Medication / supplements taken today:	
Breakfast	Lunch

Rate your worst symptoms today:

Anger ☐ Anxiety ☐ De-Motivation ☐ Depression ☐ Insomnia ☐
Irritability ☐ Misophonia ☐ Paranoia ☐ Teary ☐ Other:

..................☐ ....☐ ....☐ ....☐ ....☐

List some activities you did today:

List at least 5 things you're grateful for today:

-
-
-
-
-

Summarise your day and how you're feeling:

Day of cycle: Date: ..../......./.........

General Mood:

                                                  Other

OK / Happy	Unsure / Not Great	Angry / Raging	Emotional	

Appointments / things to do today:	
• • •	• • • • •

Medication / supplements taken today:

Breakfast	Lunch

Rate your worst symptoms today:

Anger ☐ Anxiety ☐ De-Motivation ☐ Depression ☐ Insomnia ☐
Irritability ☐ Misophonia ☐ Paranoia ☐ Teary ☐ Other:

.... ☐ .... ☐ .... ☐ .... ☐ .... ☐

List some activities you did today:

List at least 5 things you're grateful for today:

-
-
-
-
-

Summarise your day and how you're feeling:

Day of cycle: Date: ..../......./.........

General Mood:

                                                              Other

OK / Happy   Unsure /   Angry /   Emotional
                  Not Great   Raging

Appointments / things to do today: • • •	• • • • •
Medication / supplements taken today:	
Breakfast	Lunch

Rate your worst symptoms today:

Anger ☐ Anxiety ☐ De-Motivation ☐ Depression ☐ Insomnia ☐
Irritability ☐ Misophonia ☐ Paranoia ☐ Teary ☐ Other:

.... ☐ .... ☐ .... ☐ .... ☐ .... ☐

List some activities you did today:

List at least 5 things you're grateful for today:

-
-
-
-
-

Summarise your day and how you're feeling:

Day of cycle: Date: ..../......./.........

General Mood:

Other

OK / Happy	Unsure / Not Great	Angry / Raging	Emotional	

Appointments / things to do today:	•
•	•
•	•
•	•
	•

Medication / supplements taken today:

Breakfast	Lunch

Rate your worst symptoms today:

Anger ☐ Anxiety ☐ De-Motivation ☐ Depression ☐ Insomnia ☐
Irritability ☐ Misophonia ☐ Paranoia ☐ Teary ☐ Other:

................☐ ....☐ ....☐ ....☐ ....☐

List some activities you did today:

List at least 5 things you're grateful for today:

-
-
-
-
-

Summarise your day and how you're feeling:

Day of cycle: Date: ..../......./.........

General Mood:
                                                                Other

OK / Happy   Unsure /   Angry /   Emotional
                 Not Great   Raging

Appointments / things to do today:	
• • •	• • • • •
Medication / supplements taken today:	
Breakfast	Lunch
Dinner	Snacks

Rate your worst symptoms today:

Anger ☐ Anxiety ☐ De-Motivation ☐ Depression ☐ Insomnia ☐
Irritability ☐ Misophonia ☐ Paranoia ☐ Teary ☐ Other:

.............☐ ....☐ ....☐ ....☐ ....☐

List some activities you did today:

List at least 5 things you're grateful for today:

-
-
-
-
-

Summarise your day and how you're feeling:

Day of cycle: Date: ..../......./.........

General Mood:
                                                            Other

😊   🙁   😠   😭

OK / Happy   Unsure /   Angry /   Emotional
              Not Great   Raging

Appointments / things to do today:	
• • •	• • • • •

Medication / supplements taken today:

Breakfast	Lunch
Dinner	Snacks

Rate your worst symptoms today:

Anger ☐ Anxiety ☐ De-Motivation ☐ Depression ☐ Insomnia ☐
Irritability ☐ Misophonia ☐ Paranoia ☐ Teary ☐ Other:

................☐ ....☐ ....☐ ....☐ ....☐

List some activities you did today:

List at least 5 things you're grateful for today:

-
-
-
-
-

Summarise your day and how you're feeling:

Day of cycle: Date: ..../......./.........

General Mood:

                                                 Other

OK / Happy   Unsure /   Angry /   Emotional
                Not Great   Raging

Appointments / things to do today:	
• • •	• • • • •
Medication / supplements taken today:	
Breakfast	Lunch
Dinner	Snacks

Rate your worst symptoms today:

Anger ☐ Anxiety ☐ De-Motivation ☐ Depression ☐ Insomnia ☐
Irritability ☐ Misophonia ☐ Paranoia ☐ Teary ☐ Other:

...............☐ ....☐ ....☐ ....☐ ....☐

List some activities you did today:

List at least 5 things you're grateful for today:

-
-
-
-
-

Summarise your day and how you're feeling:

Day of cycle: Date: ..../......./.........

General Mood:
                                                        Other

OK / Happy   Unsure /   Angry /   Emotional
                  Not Great   Raging

Appointments / things to do today:	
• • •	• • • • •

Medication / supplements taken today:

Breakfast	Lunch
Dinner	Snacks

Rate your worst symptoms today:

Anger ☐ Anxiety ☐ De-Motivation ☐ Depression ☐ Insomnia ☐
Irritability ☐ Misophonia ☐ Paranoia ☐ Teary ☐ Other:

................☐ ....☐ ....☐ ....☐ ....☐

List some activities you did today:

List at least 5 things you're grateful for today:

-
-
-
-
-

Summarise your day and how you're feeling:

Day of cycle: Date: ..../......./.........

General Mood:

Other

OK / Happy   Unsure /   Angry /   Emotional
                  Not Great   Raging

Appointments / things to do today:	
• • •	• • • • •

Medication / supplements taken today:

Breakfast	Lunch
Dinner	Snacks

Rate your worst symptoms today:

Anger ☐ Anxiety ☐ De-Motivation ☐ Depression ☐ Insomnia ☐
Irritability ☐ Misophonia ☐ Paranoia ☐ Teary ☐ Other:

.... ☐ .... ☐ .... ☐ .... ☐ .... ☐

List some activities you did today:

List at least 5 things you're grateful for today:

-
-
-
-
-

Summarise your day and how you're feeling:

Day of cycle: _____   Date: ..../......./.........

General Mood: Other

OK / Happy   Unsure /   Angry /   Emotional
               Not Great   Raging

Appointments / things to do today:	
• • •	• • • • •
Medication / supplements taken today:	
Breakfast	Lunch
Dinner	Snacks

Rate your worst symptoms today:

Anger ☐ Anxiety ☐ De-Motivation ☐ Depression ☐ Insomnia ☐
Irritability ☐ Misophonia ☐ Paranoia ☐ Teary ☐ Other:

.... ☐ .... ☐ .... ☐ .... ☐ .... ☐

List some activities you did today:

List at least 5 things you're grateful for today:

-
-
-
-
-

Summarise your day and how you're feeling:

Day of cycle: Date: ..../......./........

General Mood:
                                                       Other

OK / Happy   Unsure /   Angry /   Emotional
              Not Great   Raging

Appointments / things to do today:	
• • •	• • • • •

Medication / supplements taken today:	

Breakfast	Lunch
Dinner	Snacks

Rate your worst symptoms today:

Anger ☐ Anxiety ☐ De-Motivation ☐ Depression ☐ Insomnia ☐
Irritability ☐ Misophonia ☐ Paranoia ☐ Teary ☐ Other:

................☐ ....☐ ....☐ ....☐ ....☐

List some activities you did today:

List at least 5 things you're grateful for today:

-
-
-
-
-

Summarise your day and how you're feeling:

Day of cycle: Date: ..../......./........

General Mood: Other

OK / Happy   Unsure /   Angry /   Emotional
              Not Great   Raging

Appointments / things to do today:	
• • •	• • • • •
Medication / supplements taken today:	
Breakfast	Lunch
Dinner	Snacks

Rate your worst symptoms today:

Anger ☐ Anxiety ☐ De-Motivation ☐ Depression ☐ Insomnia ☐
Irritability ☐ Misophonia ☐ Paranoia ☐ Teary ☐ Other:

.................☐ ....☐ ....☐ ....☐ ....☐

List some activities you did today:

List at least 5 things you're grateful for today:

-
-
-
-
-

Summarise your day and how you're feeling:

Day of cycle: Date: ..../......./.........

General Mood:

Other

OK / Happy	Unsure / Not Great	Angry / Raging	Emotional	

Appointments / things to do today:	
• • •	• • • • •

Medication / supplements taken today:	

Breakfast	Lunch
Dinner	Snacks

Rate your worst symptoms today:

Anger ☐ Anxiety ☐ De-Motivation ☐ Depression ☐ Insomnia ☐
Irritability ☐ Misophonia ☐ Paranoia ☐ Teary ☐ Other:

.............☐ ....☐ ....☐ ....☐ ....☐

List some activities you did today:

List at least 5 things you're grateful for today:

-
-
-
-
-

Summarise your day and how you're feeling:

Day of cycle: Date: ..../......./.........

General Mood: Other

OK / Happy   Unsure /   Angry /   Emotional
                  Not Great   Raging

Appointments / things to do today:	
• • •	• • • • •
Medication / supplements taken today:	
Breakfast	Lunch
Dinner	Snacks

Rate your worst symptoms today:

Anger ☐ Anxiety ☐ De-Motivation ☐ Depression ☐ Insomnia ☐
Irritability ☐ Misophonia ☐ Paranoia ☐ Teary ☐ Other:

...............☐ ....☐ ....☐ ....☐ ....☐

List some activities you did today:

List at least 5 things you're grateful for today:

-
-
-
-
-

Summarise your day and how you're feeling:

Day of cycle: Date: ..../......./........

General Mood:

                                                        Other

OK / Happy   Unsure /   Angry /   Emotional
                  Not Great   Raging

Appointments / things to do today:	
• • •	• • • • •
Medication / supplements taken today:	
Breakfast	Lunch
Dinner	Snacks

Rate your worst symptoms today:

Anger ☐ Anxiety ☐ De-Motivation ☐ Depression ☐ Insomnia ☐
Irritability ☐ Misophonia ☐ Paranoia ☐ Teary ☐ Other:

............☐ ....☐ ....☐ ....☐ ....☐

List some activities you did today:

List at least 5 things you're grateful for today:

-
-
-
-
-

Summarise your day and how you're feeling:

Day of cycle: _____   Date: ..../......./.........

General Mood:

Other

OK / Happy   Unsure /   Angry /   Emotional
                    Not Great   Raging

Appointments / things to do today:	
• • •	• • • • •

Medication / supplements taken today:

Breakfast	Lunch
Dinner	Snacks

Rate your worst symptoms today:

Anger ☐ Anxiety ☐ De-Motivation ☐ Depression ☐ Insomnia ☐
Irritability ☐ Misophonia ☐ Paranoia ☐ Teary ☐ Other:

.... ☐ .... ☐ .... ☐ .... ☐ .... ☐

List some activities you did today:

List at least 5 things you're grateful for today:

-
-
-
-
-

Summarise your day and how you're feeling:

Day of cycle:

Date: ..../......./.........

General Mood:

Other

OK / Happy
Unsure / Not Great
Angry / Raging
Emotional

Appointments / things to do today:	
• • •	• • • • •

Medication / supplements taken today:

Breakfast	Lunch
Dinner	Snacks

Rate your worst symptoms today:

Anger ☐ Anxiety ☐ De-Motivation ☐ Depression ☐ Insomnia ☐
Irritability ☐ Misophonia ☐ Paranoia ☐ Teary ☐ Other:

.... ☐ .... ☐ .... ☐ .... ☐ .... ☐

List some activities you did today:

List at least 5 things you're grateful for today:

-
-
-
-
-

Summarise your day and how you're feeling:

Day of cycle: _____   Date: ..../......./.........

General Mood:

Other

OK / Happy   Unsure /   Angry /   Emotional
              Not Great   Raging

Appointments / things to do today:	
• • •	• • • • •

Medication / supplements taken today:

Breakfast	Lunch
Dinner	Snacks

Rate your worst symptoms today:

Anger ☐ Anxiety ☐ De-Motivation ☐ Depression ☐ Insomnia ☐
Irritability ☐ Misophonia ☐ Paranoia ☐ Teary ☐ Other:

.... ☐ .... ☐ .... ☐ .... ☐ .... ☐

List some activities you did today:

List at least 5 things you're grateful for today:

-
-
-
-
-

Summarise your day and how you're feeling:

Day of cycle: Date: ..../......./.........

General Mood: Other

OK / Happy   Unsure /   Angry /   Emotional
                Not Great   Raging

Appointments / things to do today:	
• • •	• • • • •

Medication / supplements taken today:

Breakfast	Lunch
Dinner	Snacks

Rate your worst symptoms today:

Anger ☐ Anxiety ☐ De-Motivation ☐ Depression ☐ Insomnia ☐
Irritability ☐ Misophonia ☐ Paranoia ☐ Teary ☐ Other:

..................☐ ....☐ ....☐ ....☐ ....☐

List some activities you did today:

List at least 5 things you're grateful for today:

-
-
-
-
-

Summarise your day and how you're feeling:

Day of cycle: _____   Date: ..../......./.........

General Mood: Other

OK / Happy   Unsure /   Angry /   Emotional   [ ]
                  Not Great   Raging

Appointments / things to do today:	•
•	•
•	•
•	•
	•

Medication / supplements taken today:

Breakfast	Lunch
Dinner	Snacks

Rate your worst symptoms today:

Anger [ ] Anxiety [ ] De-Motivation [ ] Depression [ ] Insomnia [ ]
Irritability [ ] Misophonia [ ] Paranoia [ ] Teary [ ] Other:

...............[ ] ....[ ] ....[ ] ....[ ] ....[ ]

List some activities you did today:

List at least 5 things you're grateful for today:

-
-
-
-
-

Summarise your day and how you're feeling:

Day of cycle: Date: ..../......./.........

General Mood:

Other

OK / Happy   Unsure /   Angry /   Emotional
                  Not Great   Raging

Appointments / things to do today:	
• • •	• • • • •

Medication / supplements taken today:

Breakfast	Lunch
Dinner	Snacks

Rate your worst symptoms today:

Anger ☐ Anxiety ☐ De-Motivation ☐ Depression ☐ Insomnia ☐
Irritability ☐ Misophonia ☐ Paranoia ☐ Teary ☐ Other:

...............☐ ....☐ ....☐ ....☐ ....☐

List some activities you did today:

List at least 5 things you're grateful for today:

-
-
-
-
-

Summarise your day and how you're feeling:

Day of cycle: Date: ..../......./.........

General Mood:

Other

OK / Happy   Unsure /   Angry /   Emotional
                  Not Great   Raging

Appointments / things to do today: • • •	• • • • •
Medication / supplements taken today:	
Breakfast Dinner	Lunch Snacks

Rate your worst symptoms today:

Anger ☐ Anxiety ☐ De-Motivation ☐ Depression ☐ Insomnia ☐
Irritability ☐ Misophonia ☐ Paranoia ☐ Teary ☐ Other:

...................☐ ....☐ ....☐ ....☐ ....☐

List some activities you did today:

List at least 5 things you're grateful for today:
-
-
-
-
-

Summarise your day and how you're feeling:

Day of cycle: Date: ..../......./........

General Mood: Other

OK / Happy   Unsure /   Angry /   Emotional
              Not Great   Raging

Appointments / things to do today:	•
•	•
•	•
•	•
	•

Medication / supplements taken today:

Breakfast	Lunch
Dinner	Snacks

Rate your worst symptoms today:

Anger ☐ Anxiety ☐ De-Motivation ☐ Depression ☐ Insomnia ☐
Irritability ☐ Misophonia ☐ Paranoia ☐ Teary ☐ Other:

.... ☐ .... ☐ .... ☐ .... ☐ ....☐

List some activities you did today:

List at least 5 things you're grateful for today:

-
-
-
-
-

Summarise your day and how you're feeling:

Day of cycle: Date: ..../......./.........

General Mood:
                                                       Other

OK / Happy   Unsure /   Angry /   Emotional
                  Not Great   Raging

Appointments / things to do today:	
• • •	• • • • •

Medication / supplements taken today:

Breakfast	Lunch
Dinner	Snacks

Rate your worst symptoms today:

Anger ☐ Anxiety ☐ De-Motivation ☐ Depression ☐ Insomnia ☐
Irritability ☐ Misophonia ☐ Paranoia ☐ Teary ☐ Other:

.... ☐ .... ☐ .... ☐ .... ☐ .... ☐

List some activities you did today:

List at least 5 things you're grateful for today:

-
-
-
-
-

Summarise your day and how you're feeling:

Day of cycle: Date: ..../......./........

General Mood: Other

OK / Happy	Unsure / Not Great	Angry / Raging	Emotional	

Appointments / things to do today:	•
• • •	• • •

Medication / supplements taken today:

Breakfast	Lunch
Dinner	Snacks

Rate your worst symptoms today:

Anger ☐ Anxiety ☐ De-Motivation ☐ Depression ☐ Insomnia ☐
Irritability ☐ Misophonia ☐ Paranoia ☐ Teary ☐ Other:

..............☐ ....☐ ....☐ ....☐ ....☐

List some activities you did today:

List at least 5 things you're grateful for today:

-
-
-
-
-

Summarise your day and how you're feeling:

Day of cycle: Date: ..../......./.........

General Mood: Other

OK / Happy   Unsure /   Angry /   Emotional
              Not Great   Raging

Appointments / things to do today:	•
•	•
•	•
•	•
	•

Medication / supplements taken today:

Breakfast	Lunch
Dinner	Snacks

Rate your worst symptoms today:

Anger ☐ Anxiety ☐ De-Motivation ☐ Depression ☐ Insomnia ☐
Irritability ☐ Misophonia ☐ Paranoia ☐ Teary ☐ Other:
.............☐ ....☐ ....☐ ....☐ ....☐

List some activities you did today:

List at least 5 things you're grateful for today:

-
-
-
-
-

Summarise your day and how you're feeling:

Day of cycle: _____   Date: ..../......./.........

General Mood:

Other

OK / Happy   Unsure /   Angry /   Emotional
                  Not Great   Raging

Appointments / things to do today:	
• • •	• • • • •
Medication / supplements taken today:	
Breakfast	Lunch
Dinner	Snacks

Rate your worst symptoms today:

Anger ☐ Anxiety ☐ De-Motivation ☐ Depression ☐ Insomnia ☐
Irritability ☐ Misophonia ☐ Paranoia ☐ Teary ☐ Other:

................☐ ....☐ ....☐ ....☐ ....☐

List some activities you did today:

List at least 5 things you're grateful for today:

-
-
-
-
-

Summarise your day and how you're feeling:

Day of cycle: Date: ..../......./.........

General Mood: Other

OK / Happy   Unsure /   Angry /   Emotional
              Not Great   Raging

Appointments / things to do today:	•
	•
	•
•	•
•	•
•	

Medication / supplements taken today:

Breakfast	Lunch
Dinner	Snacks

Rate your worst symptoms today:

Anger ☐ Anxiety ☐ De-Motivation ☐ Depression ☐ Insomnia ☐
Irritability ☐ Misophonia ☐ Paranoia ☐ Teary ☐ Other:

...............☐ ....☐ ....☐ ....☐ ....☐

List some activities you did today:

List at least 5 things you're grateful for today:

-
-
-
-
-

Summarise your day and how you're feeling:

Day of cycle: Date: ..../......./.........

General Mood: Other

OK / Happy	Unsure / Not Great	Angry / Raging	Emotional	

Appointments / things to do today:	•
• • •	• • •
Medication / supplements taken today:	
Breakfast	Lunch
Dinner	Snacks

Rate your worst symptoms today:

Anger ☐ Anxiety ☐ De-Motivation ☐ Depression ☐ Insomnia ☐
Irritability ☐ Misophonia ☐ Paranoia ☐ Teary ☐ Other:

................☐ ....☐ ....☐ ....☐ ....☐

List some activities you did today:

List at least 5 things you're grateful for today:

-
-
-
-
-

Summarise your day and how you're feeling:

Day of cycle: Date: ..../......./.........

General Mood:
                                                           Other

OK / Happy   Unsure /   Angry /   Emotional
                  Not Great   Raging

Appointments / things to do today:	•
•	•
•	•
•	•
	•

Medication / supplements taken today:

| Breakfast | Lunch |
| Dinner | Snacks |

Rate your worst symptoms today:

Anger ☐ Anxiety ☐ De-Motivation ☐ Depression ☐ Insomnia ☐
Irritability ☐ Misophonia ☐ Paranoia ☐ Teary ☐ Other:

..............☐ ....☐ ....☐ ....☐ ....☐

List some activities you did today:

List at least 5 things you're grateful for today:

-
-
-
-
-

Summarise your day and how you're feeling:

Day of cycle: Date: ..../......./.........

General Mood: Other

OK / Happy | Unsure / Not Great | Angry / Raging | Emotional

Appointments / things to do today: • • •	• • • • •
Medication / supplements taken today:	
Breakfast	Lunch
Dinner	Snacks

Rate your worst symptoms today:

Anger ☐ Anxiety ☐ De-Motivation ☐ Depression ☐ Insomnia ☐
Irritability ☐ Misophonia ☐ Paranoia ☐ Teary ☐ Other:

.... ☐ .... ☐ .... ☐ .... ☐ .... ☐

List some activities you did today:

List at least 5 things you're grateful for today:

-
-
-
-
-

Summarise your day and how you're feeling:

Notes

Notes Continued

Made in the USA
Monee, IL
12 March 2022

92826112R00105